The Great
Reef Race

Leyland Perree　　　Stuart McGhee

www.glue-publishing.co.uk

All rights reserved; no part of this publication may be reproduced or transmitted by any means, electronic, mechanical, photocopying or otherwise without the prior permission of the author, illustrator and publisher.

First published in Great Britain in 2012 by Ghostly Publishing.
This edition published in Great Britain in 2015 by GLUE kids, an imprint of GLUE Publishing.

The moral right of the author has been asserted.

Visit www.glue-publishing.co.uk for more information.

Connect with the author at www.leylandperree.co.uk
Connect with the illustrator at www.stuartmcghee.com

Text Copyright © 2012 Leyland Perree
Images Copyright © 2012 Stuart McGhee
All rights reserved.
ISBN: 978-0-9931852-0-5

For Mark, Hannah, Daisy
and Isla

With love

L.P.

'Eel, wake up!' said Octopus.
Eel yawned, 'What is all this fuss?
You've just disturbed my favourite dream
Of marrying a mermaid queen.'

Ock said, 'Eel - it's finally here!
We've waited for this day all year.
So rise and shine. We don't have long.
I'll go and put the kettle on.'

Later, at the starting place...
all kinds had turned up for the race:

A cod (determined not to lose).

A crab (in nice new running shoes).

Fishy fathers, sons and daughters.

The Race Judge yelled: 'The rules are clear.
Out to the wreck, then straight back here.
No pushing. No stinging. No nipping of fins.
On your marks... get set... let the best fish win!'

From the starting stone to the finishing rock
In a blur of bubbles went Eel and Ock.
With a **wriggle** and a **jiggle** and a **giggle** they swam
Like only an eel and an octopus can.

Over, under, through and round,
They streaked along until they found
A tunnel leading through the rock.
'It's dark in here,' gulped Eel to Ock.

When the Judge was out of sight
The shark began to shove and fight
And barge his way up through the pack.
But what's that light over there in the black?

The light belonged to a Deep Sea Angler
Who lit the way with his glowy fish-dangler.
But the shark up front couldn't see at all
And crashed into the sea-cave wall.

Now that the shark was out of the race
The others were able to pick up the pace.
Out of the cave the swimmers flew.
Out of the black and into the blue.

Thrilling was the competition
As, jostling for pole-position,
The sea-slug took a fleeting lead,
But lost his way in a maze of weed.

The crab moved up to take his place
But to his horror and disgrace
He **tripped** upon a loose shoelace
And tumbled (sideways) out of the race.

Eel puffed, 'Ock, I think we're gaining!
I told you it was worth the training.
As long as we can hold our pace
Then **we** could win the Great Reef Race!'

The cod and whale were neck and neck
When the racers reached the sunken wreck
But poor old whale ran out of luck
When in the vessel he got **stuck!**

The swimmers piled up right behind,
With a BIFF! and an 'OOF!' and a 'Do you mind?'
'It's just no use,' the lobster frowned.
'He's jammed up tight. Let's go around.'

'We can't just leave him here,' said Eel.
'If that was **you**, how would you feel?'
Ock said, 'I've a plan, I think.'
'Use your head?'
'No - use my **ink!**'

And so they did as Ock had said
And inked the whale from tail to head.
They pushed and pulled and finally,
With a PLOP! the whale shot free!

WHEEEEEE! cried the whale as he sailed on past.

CRASH! went the whale knocking over the mast.

CRUNCH!

went the mast through the roof of the room where the cannons lay quiet.

What's a cannon, Ock?

Carried by the blast they sped
Away from the wreck and the seaweed bed
On past the reef with the cave underneath
(Where the shark in the dark was **still** picking up teeth).

Meanwhile, the remaining flock
Was closing on the finish rock
And in the lead, to its surprise:
A squishy thing that had no eyes!

The Race Judge waved his flag and smiled:
'It's over guys. Man, that was **wild!**
You all gave an exciting chase
But here's the **winner** of the race.'

And to the wonder of them all
He held aloft a cannonball
And clinging to it, ghostly pale,
(And still in shock) was Mark the Snail!

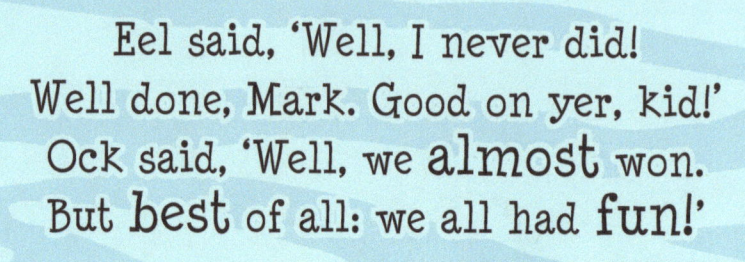

Eel said, 'Well, I never did!
Well done, Mark. Good on yer, kid!'
Ock said, 'Well, we almost won.
But best of all: we all had fun!'

Homeward from the finishing rock
Swam two **good** losers; Eel and Ock.
With a **wriggle** and a **jiggle** and a **giggle** they swam,
Like only an eel and an octopus can.

About the Author
Leyland Perree

Leyland Perree is a freelance children's author. His illustrated picture books include *Frog on the Log*, *The Goat that Gloats* and *Toad's Road Code*.

He has worked as a graphic designer, an engineer, a T-shirt printer, a sign-maker, a customer service advisor for a television company, a page-setter at a local newspaper, in a factory specialising in handmade industrial rubber goods, and as a typographer within the training industry.

He didn't get the job making authentic replica WWII flight jackets, which he still thinks would have been pretty darn cool.

Leyland lives with his wife and son in a small village on the edge of Dartmoor, forty seconds' drive from a zoo.

Visit Leyland's website for further information on works past, present and future:
www.leylandperree.co.uk

About the Illustrator
Stuart McGhee

Stuart McGhee is a freelance illustrator and cartoonist. Prior to illustrating he worked in an office shuffling paper, but after obtaining a degree in Illustration and Print from the Plymouth College of Art he is now following his dream of doodling for a living.

Stuart lives in Plymouth at the opposite end of the country to his native Scotland.

Check out his gallery of works on his website:
www.stuartmcghee.com

If you enjoyed this book by
Leyland Perree and **Stuart McGhee**
then watch out for other books from these two knuckleheads...

"Fabulous fun,
perfect for halloween"

"Quirky and fun"

"A great (and enjoyably dark)
Christmas read"

"Thoroughly caddish"

For further information, visit us at:

www.glue-publishing.co.uk

www.ingramcontent.com/pod-product-compliance
Lightning Source LLC
Chambersburg PA
CBHW042143290426
44110CB00002B/100